Doggi...

German Shepherds

ELIZABETH NOLL

BLACK
RABBIT
BOOKS

Bolt is published by Black Rabbit Books
P.O. Box 3263, Mankato, Minnesota, 56002.
www.blackrabbitbooks.com
Copyright © 2018 Black Rabbit Books

Jennifer Besel, editor; Grant Gould, interior
designer; Michael Sellner, cover designer;
Omay Ayres, photo researcher

Library of Congress Cataloging-in-Publication Data
Names: Noll, Elizabeth, author.
Title: German shepherds / by Elizabeth Noll.
Description: Mankato, Minnesota : Black Rabbit Books, [2018] | Series:
Bolt. Doggie data | Audience: Ages 9-12. | Audience: Grades 4-6. |
Includes bibliographical references and index.
Identifiers: LCCN 2016049956 (print) | LCCN 2017002154 (ebook) | ISBN
9781680721522 (library binding) | ISBN 9781680722161 (e-book) | ISBN
9781680724554 (paperback)
Subjects: LCSH: German shepherd dog–Juvenile literature.
Classification: LCC SF429.G37 N65 2018 (print) | LCC SF429.G37 (ebook)
| DDC 636.737/6-dc23
LC record available at https://lccn.loc.gov/2016049956

Printed in the United States at CG Book Printers,
North Mankato, Minnesota, 56003. 3/17

Contents

CHAPTER 1

Meet the

German Shepherd

"Help! Help!" The cries came from under a pile of **rubble**. A tornado had destroyed houses. People were trapped under collapsed walls.

A German shepherd climbed fearlessly over the mess. It sniffed here and there. Suddenly, it barked.

Rescue workers started to dig. They found a mother and two small children. The dog had saved the day.

40 50 60
30 70
20 80
10 90
0 —————— 100
pounds   **pounds**

WEIGHT
65 TO 90
POUNDS
(29 to 41 kilograms)

Smart, Hard-Working Dogs

German shepherds are often trained as rescue dogs. They are very smart. The dogs like to learn, and they like to work.

German shepherds can make good pets. But they need to be busy. If they are bored, they might cause trouble.

◄ • • • • • How Big Is a German Shepherd?

HEIGHT at shoulder
22 TO 26 INCHES
(56 to 66 centimeters)

SLOPING BACK

LONG, FLUFFY TAIL

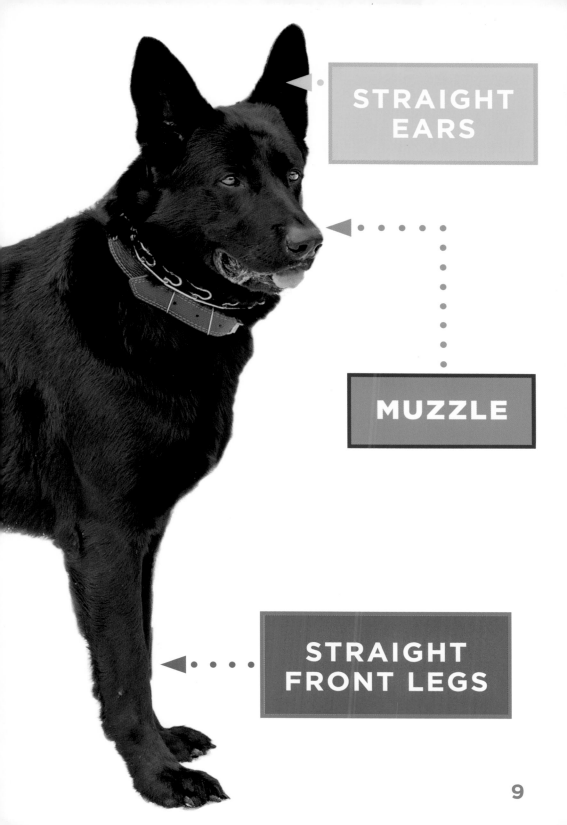

STRAIGHT
EARS

MUZZLE

STRAIGHT
FRONT LEGS

9

CHAPTER 2

A Special Personality

German shepherds are very **loyal**. They protect their owners. Sometimes they are too protective. They might bark at visitors.

It's important to train these dogs. Without training, they might bite or fight when they shouldn't.

TOP 10 MOST POPULAR Dogs in the United States in 2015

1	2	3	4
Labrador Retrievers	German Shepherds	Golden Retrievers	Bulldogs

5 Beagles

6 French Bulldogs

7 Yorkshire Terriers

8 Poodles

9 Rottweilers

10 Boxers

Good Jobs for German Shepherds

service dog

guard and
police dog

search and
rescue dog

A Shepherd's Instincts

Think about the dogs' name. "Shepherd" means "to **herd** or guide sheep." German shepherds were **bred** to run after sheep. They worked to keep sheep together.

These dogs are smart, alert, and tough. But they need jobs to do. If they get bored, they might try to herd children.

Lots of Activity

German shepherds love to be active. These dogs want to run and play. If they don't get exercise, watch out. They will chew and claw things in the house.

COMPARING SIZES

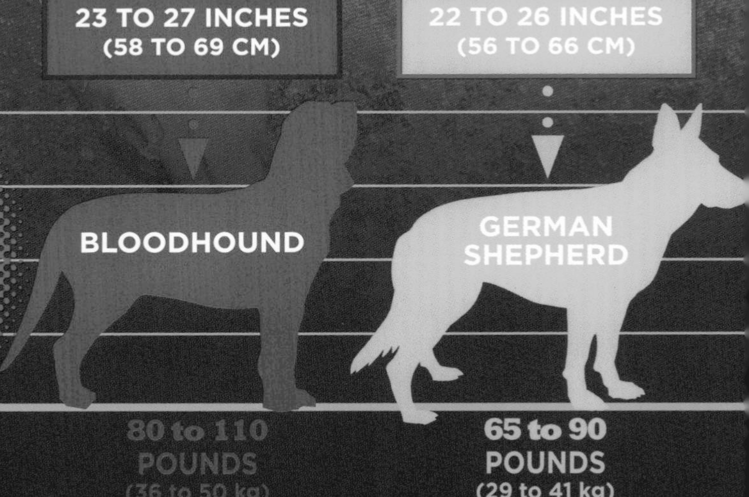

**23 TO 27 INCHES
(58 TO 69 CM)**

**22 TO 26 INCHES
(56 TO 66 CM)**

BLOODHOUND

GERMAN
SHEPHERD

**80 to 110
POUNDS**
(36 to 50 kg)

**65 to 90
POUNDS**
(29 to 41 kg)

CHAPTER 3

German Shepherds'

German shepherds are big dogs. They can weigh up to 90 pounds (41 kg).

Most German shepherds have brown and black coats. A few are solid black, gray, and even white. They have very thick hair.

13 TO 15 INCHES (33 TO 38 CM)

6 TO 9 INCHES (15 TO 23 CM)

YORKSHIRE TERRIER

BEAGLE

18 to 30 POUNDS (8 to 14 kg)

less than 7 POUNDS (3 kg)

Health Problems

German shepherds are strong and **muscular**. But these dogs can get sick. One common problem is hip **dysplasia**. With this problem, the dogs' hips don't work right. Fewer than one in five German shepherds has this problem.

1 in 5

German Shepherd

Life Cycle

A newborn puppy weighs about 1 pound (.5 kg).

PUPPY

Senior shepherds sleep more and move more slowly.

ADOLESCENT

Young German shepherds might not follow rules they followed as puppies.

ADULT

SENIOR

German shepherds are fully grown by their third birthdays.

These dogs shed a lot of hair. Their nickname is "German shedders."

 Caring

for German Shepherds

Dogs are fun. They also need to be taken care of. All dogs need regular vet checkups. German shepherds need their coats brushed regularly. They also need baths when they get dirty. Nails need to be trimmed when they get long.

Eating and Exercising

Every dog needs food and water. German shepherds are big dogs. They need a lot of food.

Dogs need exercise too. A big dog needs lots of exercise. German shepherds need one to two hours of exercise every day.

Loyal and Loving

German shepherds are loyal and loving pets. Some do come with health problems. They all need a lot of attention. But owners say their pups are worth it.

Is a German Shepherd

Right for You?

Answer the questions below. Then add up your points to see if a German shepherd is a good fit.

1 What's your favorite way to spend an hour?

A. watching TV **(1 point)**

B. going shopping **(2 points)**

C. playing outside **(3 points)**

2 What's the best size for a dog?

A. tiny (1 point)

B. medium (2 points)

C. big (3 points)

3 What kind of coat would you like your dog to have?

A. smooth and sleek (1 point)

B. curly and messy (2 points)

C. soft and thick (3 points)

{
3 points
A German shepherd is not your best match.

4–8 points
You like shepherds, but another breed might be better for you.

9 points
A German shepherd would be a great buddy for your life!
}

29

adolescent (ad-oh-LES-uhnt)—a young person or animal that is developing into an adult

breed (BREED)—the process by which young animals are produced by their parents

dysplasia (dys-PLA-zhuh)—an abnormal structure

herd (HURD)—to gather and move animals or people into a group

loyal (LOY-uhl)—having complete support for someone or something

muscular (MUS-kyu-lur)—having large and strong muscles

muzzle (MUH-zuhl)—the usually long nose and mouth of an animal

rubble (RUH-buhl)—broken pieces of stone or other materials from buildings that have fallen

BOOKS

Bodden, Valerie. *German Shepherds.* Fetch! Mankato, MN: Creative Education, 2014.

Bowman, Chris. *German Shepherds.* Awesome Dogs. Minneapolis: Bellwether Media, 2016.

Gray, Susan H. *German Shepherds.* All About Dogs. New York: AV2 by Weigl, 2017.

WEBSITES

German Shepherd
www.animalplanet.com/tv-shows/dogs-101/videos/german-shepherd/

German Shepherd (GSD) Dog Breed Information
www.akc.org/dog-breeds/german-shepherd-dog/

German Shepherd Dog Club of America
www.gsdca.org

INDEX